Where are the ROYAL FAMILY?

Can you find the British Monarchy?

igloobooks

Where are the ROYAL FAMILY?

Can you find the British Monarchy?

Why do people love the British Royal Family? All around the world, they're treated like celebrities, and many of them have celebrity friends of their own. The media loves to report on them: where they've been, who they've seen, even what they were wearing. They're British icons, just like afternoon tea and cricket.

Of course, the Royal Family are expected to conduct themselves properly as representatives of the Queen and Country. Whether they're attending a royal wedding, a coronation, or the changing of the guard, all eyes are on them, and so they love to unwind at the end of a long day. Perhaps you'll find the queen admiring the crown jewels, or even trying on a few new hats.

Prince Charles was in the Navy, so he might be relaxing at the regatta and watching all the boats. Prince William and Harry enjoy a summer garden party, so they could be joining in with the fun and games. Dancing the night away at a ball is just the ticket for Kate and Meghan, so it's possible you'll spot them on the dance floor.

Grab your crown and corgi to join the aristocracy in their celebrations, and see who else you can find on the way!

Who can you spot...?

Queen Elizabeth II
The matriarch and leading member of the British monarchy, Her Majesty Queen Elizabeth II has reigned since 1952, making her the longest-reigning living monarch in the world.

Prince Philip
The Duke of Edinburgh is the Queen's husband and known for his blunt and down-to-earth manner of speaking, as well as for his often-edgy jokes and conversations.

Camilla Parker-Bowles
Known as the Duchess of Cornwall, Camilla is the second wife of Prince Charles. She is an advocate of animal welfare, promotes global literacy, and supports many other charities.

Prince Charles
The Prince of Wales is the oldest child of Elizabeth II and heir to the British throne.

Prince William
The Duke of Cambridge is the oldest son of Prince Charles and second in line to the throne.

Meghan Markle
Before marrying Prince Harry, Meghan was a successful actress, appearing on TV and in movies.

Prince Harry
The Duke of Sussex is the younger son of Prince Charles, and had a successful army career before his retirement.

Kate Middleton
Kate is married to Prince William and, as well as accompanying her husband in his endeavors, works with charities that focus on young children, art, addiction, and mental health.

Princess Beatrice

Princess Margaret

Princess Eugenie

Queen Elizabeth, the Queen Mother

Royal Wedding

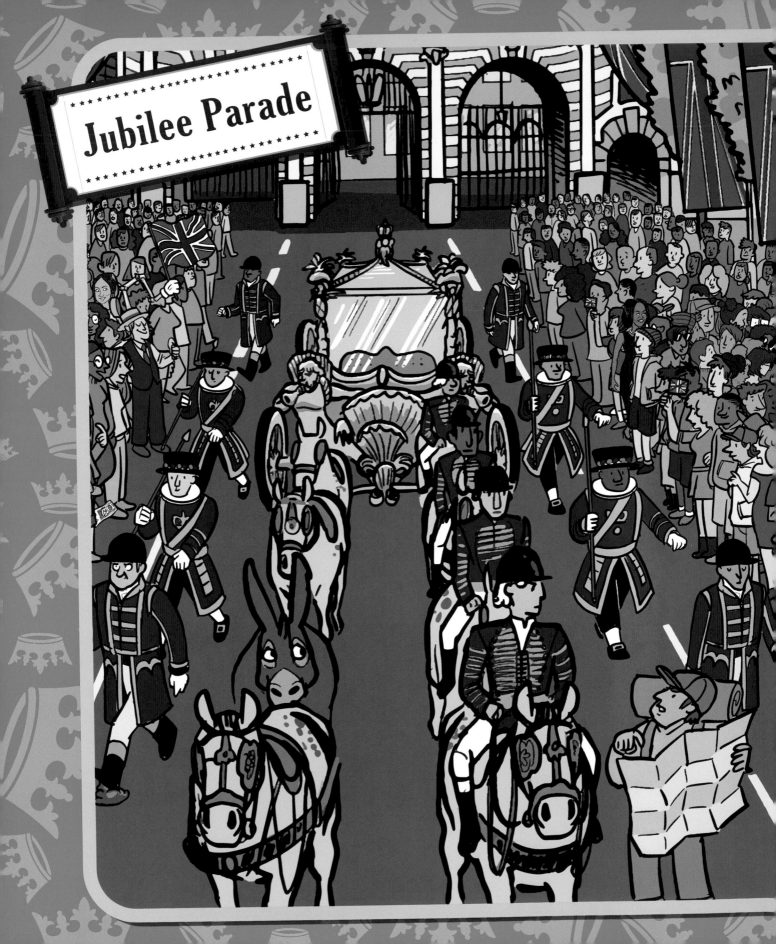

Jubilee Parade

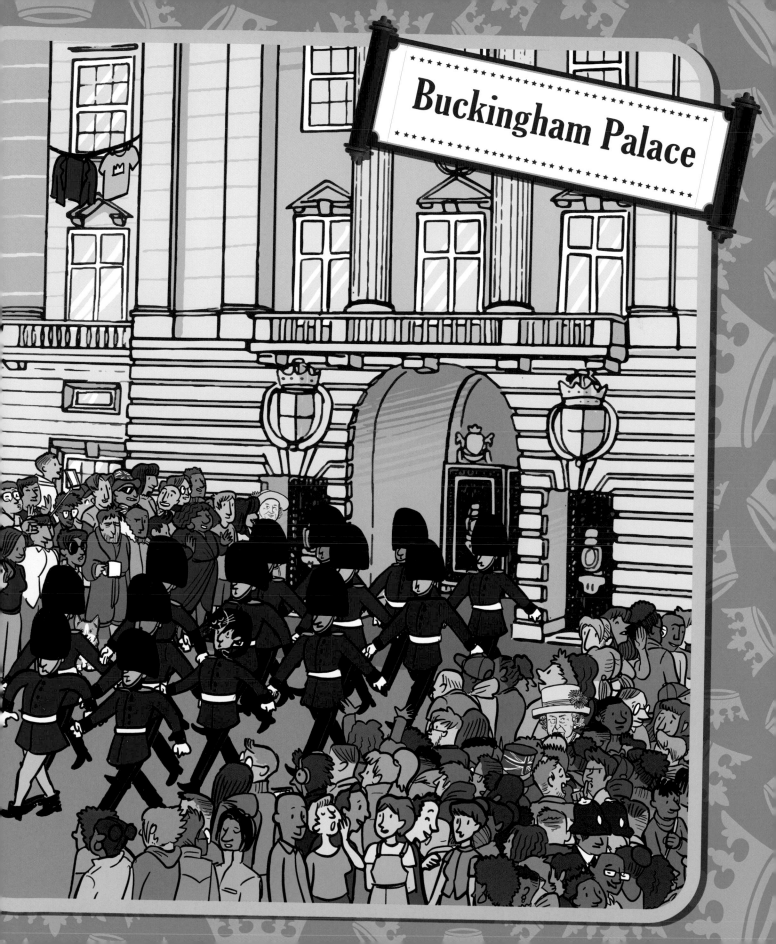

Buckingham Palace

Royal Ball

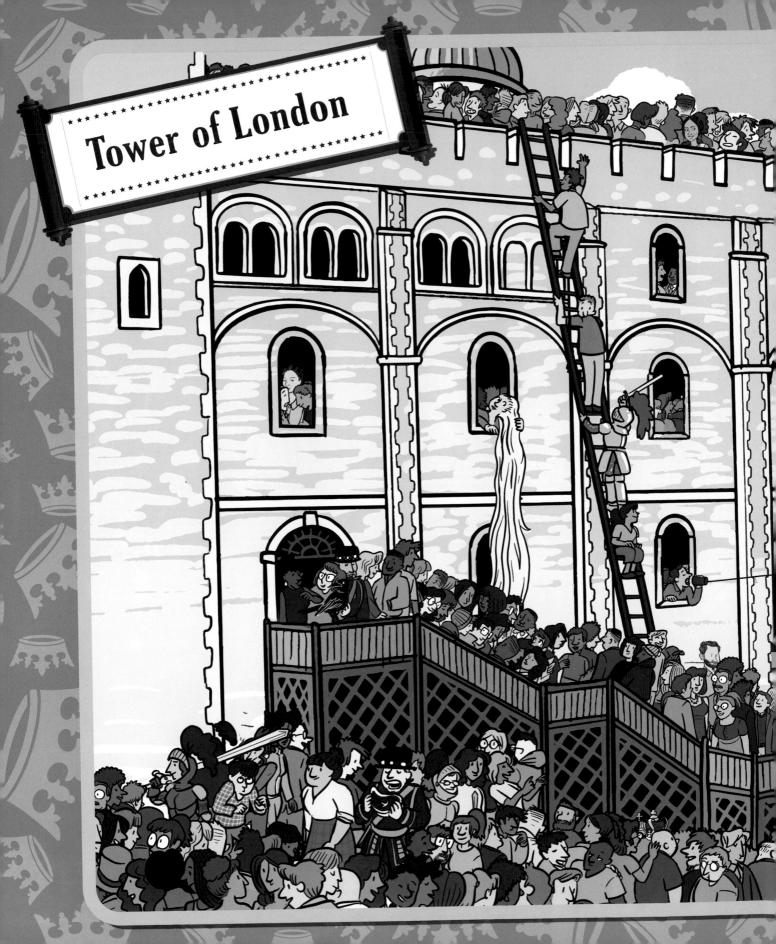

Tower of London

At the Races

Garden Party

Royal Regatta

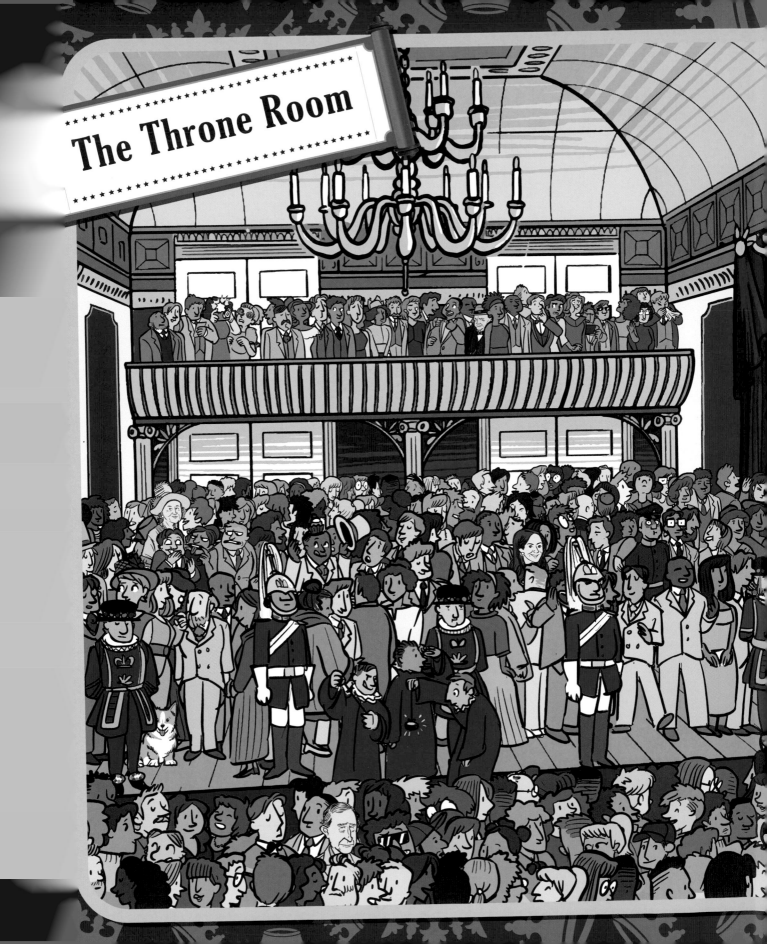

The Throne Room

Did you also spot...?

William Shakespeare —
The Bard wrote the histories of kings and queens. He even wrote for Elizabeth I!

Winston Churchill —
Famous for his leadership in World War II, Winston Churchill served as Prime Minister for both Queen Elizabeth II and her father.

Queen Victoria —
The great-great-grandmother of Elizabeth II, Victoria had the longest reign of any British monarch until her great-great-granddaughter set a new record.

Zara and Mike Tindall —
Zara is the daughter of Princess Anne and the eldest granddaughter of Queen Elizabeth II. She's an Olympic medal-winning horsewoman, and her husband is a sporting legend too; he played rugby for England!

Henry VIII —
Good King Hal was full of beans, he married half a dozen queens... then divorced two of them, and beheaded two more! The father of Elizabeth I, he's one of England's most famous monarchs.

Oprah Winfrey —
American TV royalty herself, Oprah is considered by some to be a friend of the family. She's worked with both Prince Harry and Meghan, and attended their wedding.

Pippa Middleton —
The younger sister of Kate, Pippa caught the public's attention during her sister's wedding to Prince William.

Elizabeth I —
Elizabeth I ruled for almost 45 years, saw off a Spanish Armada, and had a country named after her. Known as the Virgin Queen, she had no children, but her legacy lives on today.

Barack and Michelle Obama —
This presidential couple have met the royals on several occasions and become friends with a few of them, remaining in contact since Barack's term in office.

Sir Elton John —
Elton and the royals go way back. The singer has performed for them on numerous occasions, and lent Harry and Meghan use of his private jet.